MW01174835

Notes to the Fairy

THe Fairy is
watching you!!
Emma

Enjoy!
Your Fairy Godmother

Is your MIND Magic?
Love, Laurie Zallen

Notes to the Fairy

Emma L. Niden

and

Lisa Finneran Niden

Illustrated by Laurie Zallen

**Andrews McMeel
Publishing**

Kansas City

Notes to the Fairy

05 06 07 08 09 TWP 10 9 8 7 6 5 4 3 2 1

ISBN-13: 978-0-7407-5568-2
ISBN-10: 0-7407-5568-4

Library of Congress Control Number: 2005923691

For my father, Tom.

— L.F.N.

To Izzy, Sam, Noah, and Mary.

— L.Z.

Notes to the Fairy

Dear Tooth Fairy,

I pulled my first tooth out tonight.
Please bring me a dragon.

When dogs lose their teeth do you give them money?

Have you found my dragon?
I'd also like a star.

Please put it in my tooth fairy box, then get in.

P.S.

Do you work for Cinderella?

The next time my tooth comes out I'd like a hammer . . .

to get the dollars out of the glass paperweight on my grandfather's desk.

I call him Pa.

Can I try out your wand?

Leave it under my pillow.

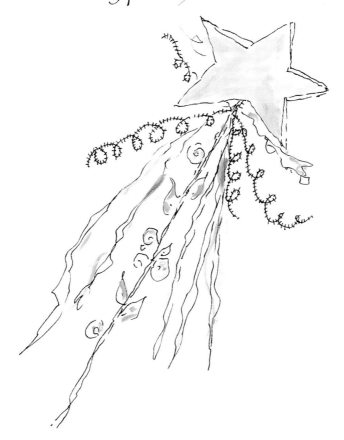

I want a magic spell book.

P.S.

Do crickets have noses?

If I eat a blade of grass will
I be summer inside?

I want the wand.

If you get it I will draw a picture of me and my teeth
at the dentist, and you can hang it up
in your castle.

P.S.

Who invented no?

I put salmon scales on my legs so my skin will soak them up and I will be a mermaid.

Also, do you have a phone?

When I'm a mermaid will I have to wear those bras made out of shells?

I'm not angry or mad, just disappointed you're so late with my stuff.

P.S. What is your name?

Can you blow on my hand and wake me up?
I won't tell anybody.

Tooth Fairy,

Here's another tooth. I would like a magic diamond crystal ball that takes me to another land.

If you do find the dragon,
I'll give you two pennies.

P.S.

Pa died.

I want wings.

Make my tooth come out at pottery camp.

Did you find the dragon, because I have the money.

Can you please give me a magic crown so when I wear it I can be older and skip childhood?

P.S.

And some new sparkly jewelry.

When a person's heart breaks does someone smash it in half with an ax?

Thank you for the crown. What does it do?
Make you smart?

Or does it make you big . . .

or small again?

Or does it make you magic . . .

or does it make you have long hair, because if it does I will wear the crown every night.

One more thing, tooth fairy,

can I see you someday?

Fairy,

I'd like a small trident.

If my mother screams her head off,

will it stay on her neck?

Here's one more tooth. I want the dragon.

When will the wings sprout?

I have a phone.

*Why all the teeth? What do you do,
build things?*

P.S.

Where's my stuff?

I'd like to come to your castle, but I need a car.

If you cut open a dead person's head,
do numbers and letters fall out?

May I please have a bird egg so I can lay my own?

Is Pa in the wind?

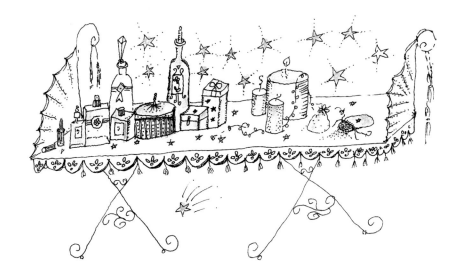

I would like a fairy kit.

Can you see in the rain?

I love the headband,

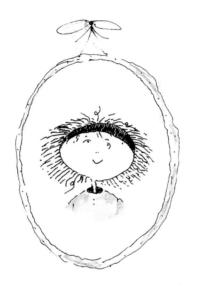

but please . . .

no more hair things.

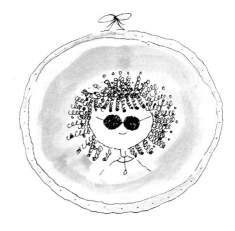

Sprinkle magic dust on my legs.

If you can't find the star, the trident,
the magic diamond crystal ball,
the egg, or the dragon . . .

please bring me a toothbrush.

P.S.

How come I have no more wiggly teeth?

Does Santa have a phone?

Dear Fairy,

My mind is magic.